#1 you must answer every question & explain why! No matter how silly or hard it may be! ENJOY

2019

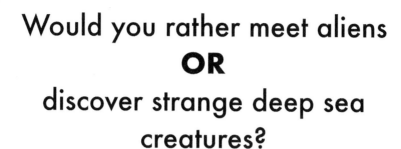

Would you rather meet aliens
OR
discover strange deep sea creatures?

Would you rather spend a whole year without daylight
OR
stand under the sun without protection for a whole week?

Would you rather have homework
OR
reading assignments?

Would you rather drink a whole glass of vinegar once
OR
only drink water for five whole years?

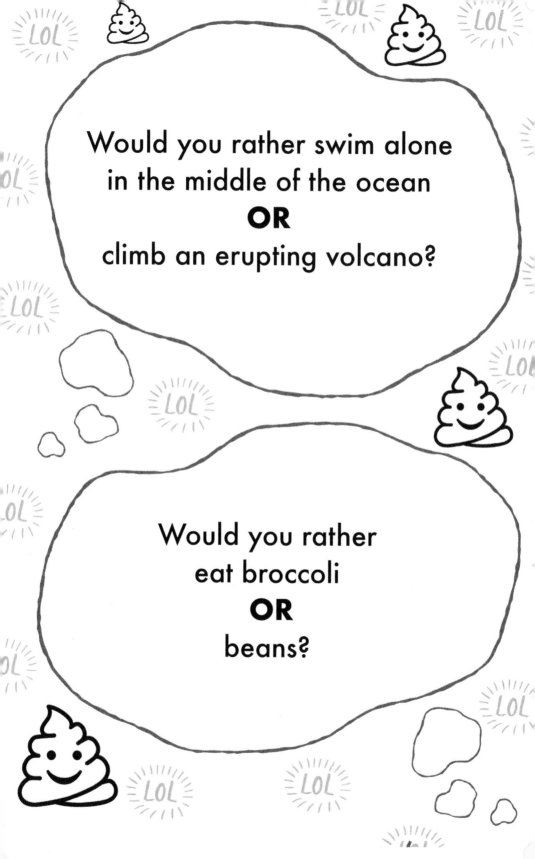

Would you rather swim alone in the middle of the ocean **OR** climb an erupting volcano?

Would you rather eat broccoli **OR** beans?

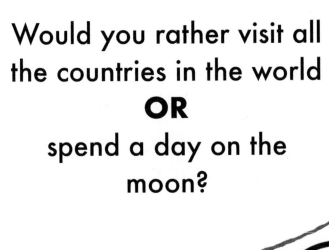

Would you rather visit all the countries in the world **OR** spend a day on the moon?

Would you rather have five arms **OR** five legs?

Would you rather play music
OR
listen to music?

Would you rather wear long pants in the middle of summer
OR
no pants at all in the middle of winter?

Would you rather
wear neon green
overalls
OR
bleach your hair an
electric blue?

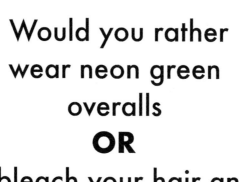

Would you rather
pet a little kitten
OR
a majestic tiger?

Would you rather eat a
cooked lizard
OR
drink juice made from
lizards ?

Would you rather have
nightmares
OR
not sleep at all?

Would you rather be a mortal billionaire **OR** someone with superpowers who only has enough to live by?

Would you rather be a doctor **OR** a vet?

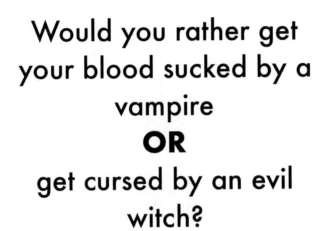

Would you rather get your blood sucked by a vampire
OR
get cursed by an evil witch?

Would you rather get struck by lightning and come out alive
OR
never be in the presence of rain ever again?

Would you rather be able
to sing amazingly
OR
dance amazingly?

Would you rather meet a
kind ogre
OR
a mean fairy?

Would you rather go back in time **OR** travel to the future?

Would you rather have 4-inch-long nails **OR** extremely crooked teeth?

Would you rather live in a museum where things come alive at night **OR** a multi storey toy store?

Would you rather spend the night alone at art gallery **OR** at an antique shop?

Would you rather sleep with
five blankets on
OR
no blankets at all?

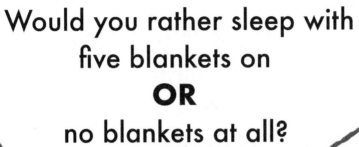

Would you rather go a
whole week without
showering
OR
brushing your teeth?

Would you rather write
stories
OR
read them?

Would you rather build a
sand castle
OR
visit a real castle?

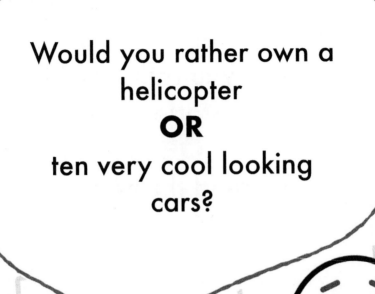

Would you rather own a helicopter
OR
ten very cool looking cars?

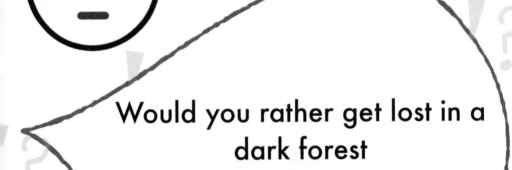

Would you rather get lost in a dark forest
OR
a labyrinth?

Would you rather live
in a vast desert
OR
a tiny island?

Would you rather
befriend a talking slug
OR a human-sized
worm?

Would you rather go camping in the woods where a bear lives
OR
in your backyard where 20 BIG harmless spiders live?

Would you rather sleep with the lights on forever
OR
have a cold shower forever?

Would you rather visit polar bears in the North Pole **OR** penguins in the South Pole?

Would you rather dive to the bottom of the ocean **OR** never touch the sea forever?

Would you rather dive to the bottom of the ocean
OR
never touch the sea forever?

Would you rather be a mermaid stuck under the sea
OR
a princess stuck in a tower?

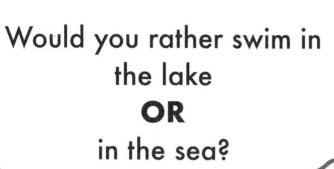

Would you rather swim in the lake
OR
in the sea?

Would you rather have more peanut butter
OR
more jelly in your PB&J's?

Would you rather lose a toy
OR
miss your favorite TV show?

Would you rather go
apple-picking
OR
make apple pie?

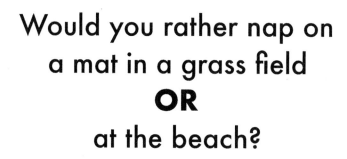

Would you rather nap on
a mat in a grass field
OR
at the beach?

Would you rather have
wings but no ability to fly
OR
horns on your head & are
able to fly?

Would you rather grant wishes
OR
make them?

Would you rather go into war with twenty capable soldiers
OR
a thousand weak ones?

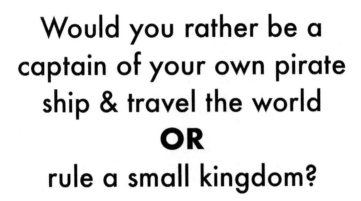

Would you rather be a
captain of your own pirate
ship & travel the world
OR
rule a small kingdom?

Would you rather fight
zombies
OR
the kraken?

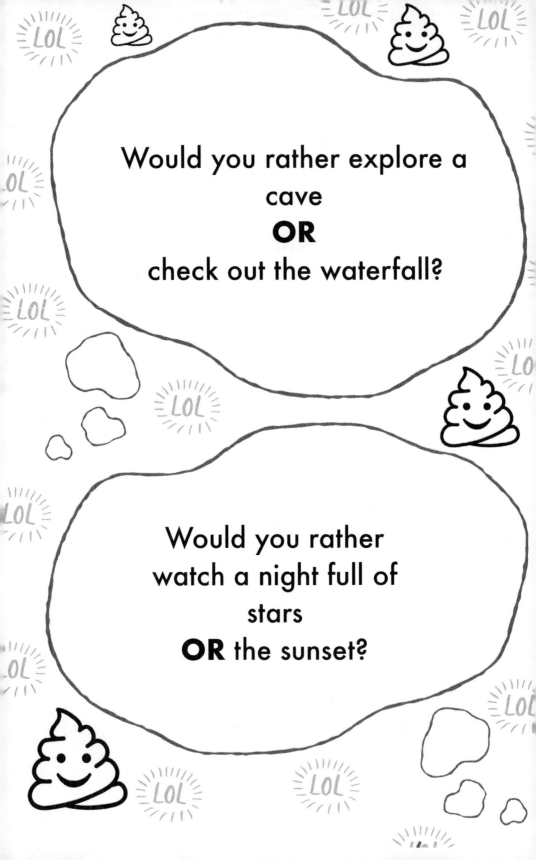

Would you rather tell
a white lie
OR
the painful truth?

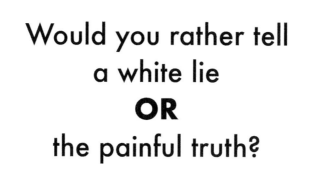

Would you rather learn ten
languages
OR
ten decades of world
history?

Would you rather wash
the dishes
OR
sweep the floor?

Would you rather wear
fluffy character socks
OR
soft cartoon pajamas?

Would you rather be chased
by a thousand angry bees
OR
one very angry Mom?

Would you rather be
an expert at one thing
OR
a jack of all trades?

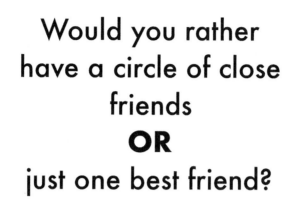

Would you rather
have a circle of close
friends
OR
just one best friend?

Would you rather fail an
exam
OR
lose a friend?

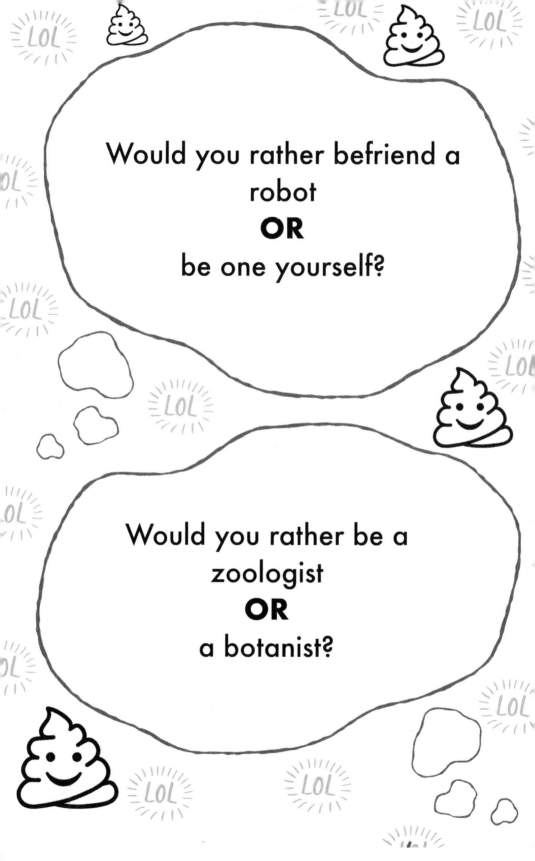

Would you rather befriend a robot
OR
be one yourself?

Would you rather be a zoologist
OR
a botanist?

Would you rather have to never wait for your meal at a restaurant ever again and pay double
OR
have infinite money but have to wait at least two hours for every meal?

Would you rather teach yourself to speak in animal language
OR
teach animals to speak in human language?

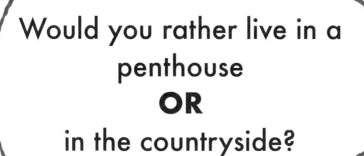

Would you rather live in a
penthouse
OR
in the countryside?

Would you rather be your
current age forever
OR
age twice as fast?

Would you rather dive into the swimming pool from a great height **OR** go down the slide with a blindfold on?

Would you rather have a swimming pool in your backyard **OR** a roller coaster?

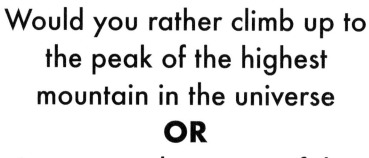

Would you rather climb up to the peak of the highest mountain in the universe
OR
journey to the center of the Earth?

Would you rather be invisible
OR
have superhuman speed?

Would you rather go
to school
OR
have a job?

Would you rather read a 500-
page book full of pictures
OR
a 20-page book with no
pictures at all?

Would you rather be made of metal **OR** cotton?

Would you rather be able to control fire **OR** water?

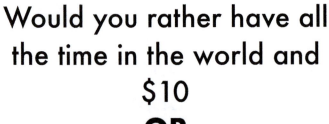

Would you rather have all the time in the world and $10 **OR** all the money in the world and 10 years?

Would you rather be able to draw anything into existence **OR** erase anything from existence?

Would you rather play games on your cell phone
OR
on your computer?

Would you rather wear flippers permanently
OR
have a hook as one of your hands?

Would you rather live in a world where all the roads are neon bright
OR
one where all the buildings are only black and white?

Would you rather have whiskers
OR
a tail?

Would you rather go through the trouble of saving the Earth
OR
escape to a planet many years away with no guarantee of survival?

Would you rather be generous to everyone you meet
OR
have everyone you meet be generous to you?

Would you rather never go bankrupt **OR** have a "Get Out of Jail Free" card that never expires?

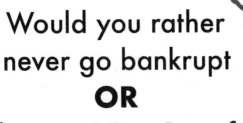

Would you rather get stung by a bee **OR** get ten mosquito bites?

Would you rather have horrible bed hair that cannot be styled forever
OR
sleep only three hours a day forever?

Would you rather be the richest person in the world
OR
the healthiest?

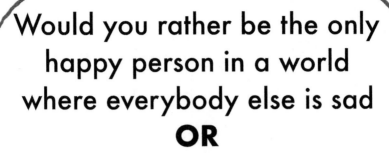

Would you rather be the only happy person in a world where everybody else is sad
OR
be the only sad person in a world where everybody else is happy?

Would you rather cry happy tears
OR
smile even when you're sad?

Would you rather live in a tiny space with too many other people **OR** live in an enormous space alone?

Would you rather live in a world where every single person knows and hates you **OR** one where not a single person knows you exist?

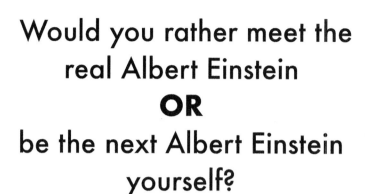

Would you rather meet the real Albert Einstein **OR** be the next Albert Einstein yourself?

Would you rather teach ten people who will later grow up to be geniuses **OR** be a genius yourself?

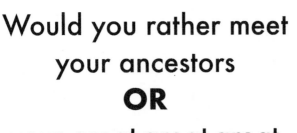

Would you rather meet
your ancestors
OR
your great-great-great-
grandchildren?

Would you rather have a
dragon
OR
a phoenix for a pet?

Would you rather have a bathroom that always leaks
OR
one with never enough water?

Would you rather grow a vegetable farm
OR
raise cattle?

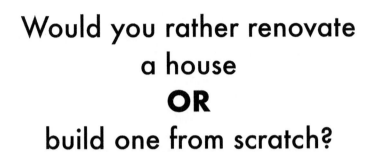

Would you rather renovate
a house
OR
build one from scratch?

Would you rather make
your parents proud
OR
make yourself happy?

Would you rather do something you like in return for little pay **OR** do something you hate for a lot of money?

Would you rather be a 150-year-old tree that can see and hear everything **OR** a 150-year-old sea turtle?

Would you rather have a beautiful house and rubbish fashion sense **OR** dress like you've just stepped out of a famous instagrammers feed?

Would you rather have the perfect instagram feed and have no fun **OR** no likes online & have an awesome life?

Would you rather be a knight
OR
a scholar in the medieval era?

Would you rather live in a world where it's night forever
OR
one where it's day forever?

Would you rather never eat any kind of bread ever again
OR
have to eat only bread forever?

Would you rather be a superhero
OR
a supervillain?

Would you rather prick your finger on a spindle of a spinning wheel and sleep forever
OR
turn into a frog prince?

Would you rather invent the smartest computer in the world
OR
be the smartest person in the world?

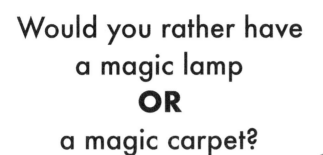

Would you rather have
a magic lamp
OR
a magic carpet?

Would you rather go on an
adventure for free
OR
stay at home with a million
dollars?

Would you rather have
a barbecue at a
camping site
OR
a picnic by the lake?

Would you rather have
an evil twin
OR
an evil stepmother?

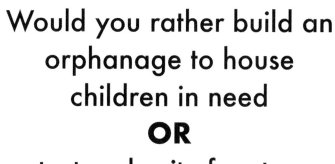

Would you rather build an orphanage to house children in need
OR
start a charity for stray animals?

Would you rather have a doll that moves and walks
OR
one that talks?

Would you rather take all of your friend's toys **OR** give them all of yours?

Would you rather be stuck in a giant whale's stomach **OR** be a wooden puppet who comes alive twice a week?

Would you rather get one birthday present **OR** a hundred birthday cards?

Would you rather hold a tarantula in your hands **OR** have a snake around your neck?

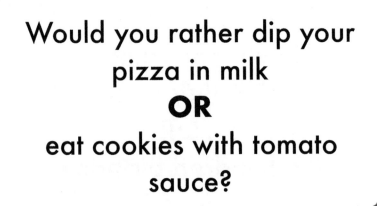

Would you rather dip your
pizza in milk
OR
eat cookies with tomato
sauce?

Would you rather
roll in wet mud
OR
eat a teaspoon of
sand?

Would you rather visit
Hogwarts
OR
Willy Wonka's chocolate
factory?

Would you rather get
something stuck in your
teeth
OR
a booger hanging out of
your nostril?

Would you rather never see a
sunset ever again
OR
never see a sunrise again?

Would you rather set out on an
archaeological mission
OR
an expedition to the poles?

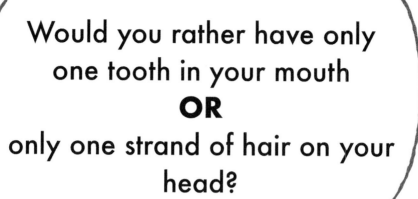

Would you rather have only one tooth in your mouth
OR
only one strand of hair on your head?

Would you rather bite your tongue
OR
stub you little toe?

Would you rather join
a choir
OR
a band?

Would you rather be an
outstanding pianist who cannot
compose music
OR
a composer who can
not play the piano?

Would you rather have hiccups for a whole day **OR** have a runny nose for a whole month?

Would you rather cast a spell on someone **OR** be cast a spell by someone?

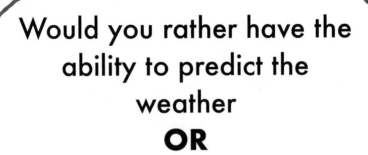

Would you rather have the ability to predict the weather
OR
predict the next sentence someone else is going to say?

Would you rather hide in the shadows
OR
stand in the spotlight?

Would you rather have a beard so long it trips you up
OR
eyelashes so long they clump together when you blink?

Would you rather have a neck as long as a giraffe's
OR
a nose as long as an elephant's?

Would you rather eat a poisonous plant **OR** be bitten by a venomous snake?

Would you rather eat your pancakes in soup **OR** drench your mushrooms in maple syrup?

Would you rather fight a
monster
OR
a feisty little elf?

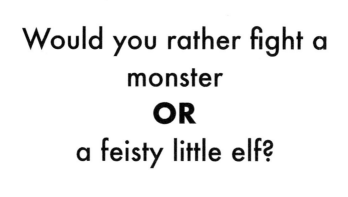

Would you rather
not talk forever
OR
never stop talking?

Would you rather be the person who breaks the promise
OR
the one whose promise is broken?

Would you rather fly on a broomstick
OR
slide down a rainbow?

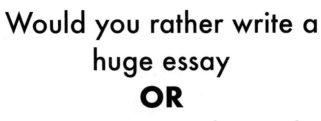

Would you rather write a huge essay
OR
recite a poem in front of a huge audience?

Would you rather pose in front of a camera
OR
be the one taking photos?

Would you rather wear a shirt with a huge stain
OR
walk around with only one shoe?

Would you rather be a soccer ball that gets kicked around
OR
a shuttlecock that gets smacked repeatedly?

Would you rather be a monkey who can speak the human language
OR
be a person who can only speak monkey?

Would you rather have the ability to understand your pet
OR
have your pet understand you?

Would you rather have fangs
OR
pointy ears?

Would you rather have a magic wand
OR
a sword that can cut through anything?

Would you rather have your face printed on a stamp
OR
a postcard?

Would you rather make the largest snowman in the world
OR
meet a yeti?

Would you rather fart very loudly in front of all your friends
OR
pee your pants?

Would you rather have to finish an entire birthday cake all by yourself
OR
not get any cake on your birthday at all?

Would you rather
sound like a trumpet
OR
an untuned guitar?

Would you
rather eat
lipstick
OR
face powder?

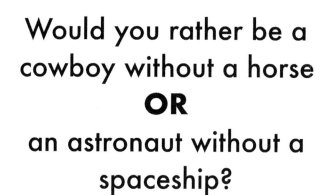

Would you rather be a cowboy without a horse **OR** an astronaut without a spaceship?

Would you rather give the wrong answer in class **OR** call your teacher Mom?

Would you rather be a black and white flamingo **OR** a pink penguin?

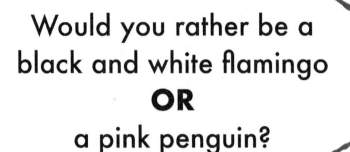

Would you rather be tangled in a truck-sized spider web **OR** meet the dog-sized spider that spun it?

Would you rather take a guaranteed $150,000 **OR** take a 50/50 chance at 1 million dollars?

Would you rather be only able to shout **OR** only be able to whisper?

Would you rather be an elephant-sized mouse **OR** a mouse-sized elephant?

Would you rather be an awesome player on the losing team **OR** the worst player on the winning team?

Would you rather drink tomato sauce **OR** dip your fries in tomato juice

Would you rather be stuck in a large bubble alone while everyone else is outside of it **OR** have bubbles come out of your mouth whenever you speak?

Would you rather
live in a giant lettuce
house
OR
a tiny rocket?

Would you rather
wear sandals to a ski
resort
OR
snow gear to the
beach?

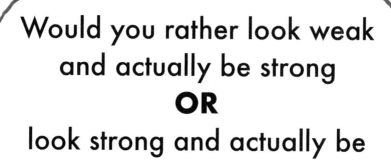

Would you rather look weak and actually be strong
OR
look strong and actually be weak?

Would you rather be invited to only one birthday party
OR
have only one friend show up to your birthday party?

Would you rather
have glow-in-the-
dark eyes
OR
glow-in-the-dark
teeth?

Would you rather write 200
would-you-rather's
OR
eat only jelly for a whole
week?

Would you rather.....................
....
....
OR...
....
....

Would you rather.....................
....
....
OR...
....

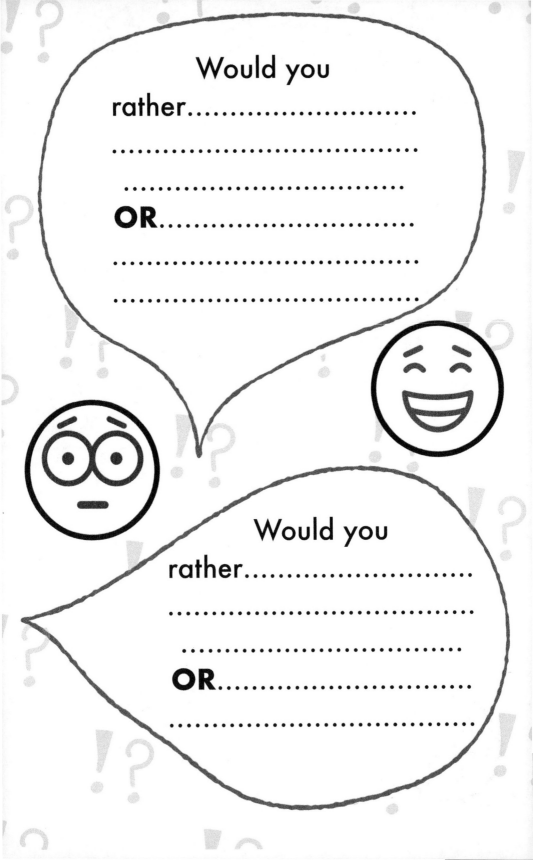

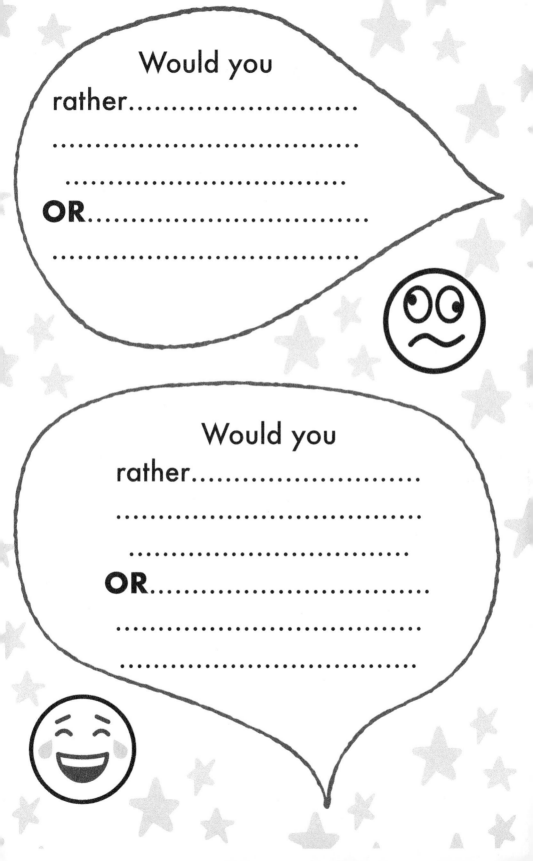

Would you rather..........................
....
....
OR.................................
....

Would you rather...........................
....
....
OR..................................
....
....

Printed in Great Britain
by Amazon

33660077R00061